EXPLORING THE DIVERSE LANDSCAPES AND CULTURES OF CANADA

EXPLORING THE DIVERSE LANDSCAPES AND CULTURES OF CANADA

ARIA NIGHTINGALE

CONTENTS

1 Introduction to Canada's Geographic and Cultural D   1
2 Historical Overview of Canada's Settlement and Dev   3
3 The Indigenous Peoples of Canada: Heritage and Con   5
4 The Canadian Constitution and Political System   7
5 Canada's Provinces and Territories: Unique Charact   9
6 The Role of French and English Languages in Canadi   11
7 Canada's Economy: Industries and Trade Partners   13
8 Canadian Arts and Literature: Influences and Notab   15
9 Exploring Canada's Natural Wonders: National Parks   17
10 The Arctic Region: Climate, Wildlife, and Indigeno   19
11 The Rocky Mountains: Geology, Flora, and Outdoor A   21
12 The Great Lakes: Ecosystems, Shipping, and Recreat   23
13 The Atlantic Provinces: Fisheries, Culture, and To   25
14 The Pacific Coast: Rainforests, Marine Life, and I   27
15 Urban Centers in Canada: Toronto, Montreal, Vancou   29
16 Multiculturalism in Canada: Immigration Patterns a   31

17	Education in Canada: Schools, Universities, and Re	33
18	Healthcare System in Canada: Universal Coverage an	35
19	Canadian Cuisine: Regional Specialties and Influen	37
20	Sports and Recreation in Canada: Popular Activitie	39
21	Transportation in Canada: Roads, Railways, and Air	41
22	Environmental Issues in Canada: Climate Change and	43
23	Indigenous Rights and Reconciliation in Canada	45
24	International Relations: Canada's Role in Global A	47
25	Innovations and Technologies in Canada: Achievemen 51	
26	The Canadian Identity: Values, Symbols, and Nation	53
27	Conclusion: Reflecting on Canada's Past, Present,	55

Copyright © 2024 by Aria Nightingale

All rights reserved. No part of this book may be reproduced in any manner whatsoever without written permission except in the case of brief quotations embodied in critical articles and reviews.

First Printing, 2024

CHAPTER 1

Introduction to Canada's Geographic and Cultural D

In Canada, you will find a land of diverse landscapes, from freshwater rivers, islands, and tundras in the north, to the boreal forests, jagged mountain ranges, deserts, and the Pacific, Atlantic, and Arctic oceans. Residents of this sparsely populated country are also diverse. While French and English are the official languages at the federal level, many more languages are spoken at the local level. The majority of residents live within range of the U.S. border, and the country's proximity to the United States has ensured an intertwined popular culture, though there are many differences. Not all Canadians prefer hockey to other sports, in the way a few don't like maple syrup! No two Canadians are exactly alike, just as no two cities are the same. Learn about Canada – from sea to sky and every place in-between.

In an attempt to showcase the rich tapestry of people and places that make up Canada, we have put together an issue with multiple sections focusing on the diversity to be found throughout the country. Often the divisions between the various regions are geographical – mountain ranges, coastlines, and the weather systems. But the diversity extends into the culture, the dependence on natural resources, the cuisine, and every other thing that makes a place unique. Join us on the following journey, exploring the edge of the ocean's waves in Newfoundland & Labrador in Atlantic Canada, while discovering the rivers, lakes, and wildlife in the heart of the country. For adventure and the majestic mountains, we explore the Rockies in Western Canada and head up the Sea to Sky area towards Northern BC. Discover why the vast and remote prairies are some of the best places to stargaze in the world and the more discerning wine expert can dive into the Okanagan's rich wine region.

CHAPTER 2

Historical Overview of Canada's Settlement and Dev

Unlike many countries, Canada did not develop as a nation over centuries. Instead, the country was gradually populated by different groups, or 'waves,' in response to social, geographic, and political factors. The toponym 'Canada' itself seems to suggest an Indigenous term used by Jacques Cartier to refer to the land. England, France, Norway, and Russia competed for ownership of the northern New World, and the first European exploration and trapping began in the late 1500s. However, Canadian expansion was a result of reactions and the influx of mass migrants into the northeastern United States, as the original migrants moved west in search of agricultural land, not as part of a deliberate plan. As a result, large sections of the West and North were never inhabited by earlier European arrivals, and they only became part of the nation by default in the early 20th century.

Apart from ancient peoples, such as the Cree, the Inuit, and the Blackfoot, Canada was first explored by Europeans in the late 15th century. The first established fort was Fort First, established in 1535 by Jacques Cartier in Stadacona (present-day Quebec City); the first

European settlement was created in Port Royal in 1605 on the banks of the Annapolis River near present-day Annapolis, Nova Scotia, by Pierre du Gua and Samuel de Champlain. However, due to poor planning, technical uncertainties, and several wars, Canada's early colonial attempts faced difficulties. A blend of French, Breton, Anglo-Norman, and Norman influences evolved over the centuries into modern-day Québécois in the St. Lawrence Valley, not only following the arrival of British and American colonists. Prior to the American Revolution of 1776, the country was limited to the Atlantic coast and the southern bank of the St. Lawrence.

CHAPTER 3

The Indigenous Peoples of Canada: Heritage and Con

Canada's communities feature vibrant strands of culture ranging from the First Nations, Inuit, and Métis: indigenous peoples that have deep connections to the country's land. Indigenous history in Canada provides an alternative historical perspective that is just as indispensable and important as the story of the colonies. Archaeological findings have traces of the presence of human habitation 12,000 years ago. Indigenous knowledge and resources administered by their era on Turtle Island remain invaluable today. Indigenous contributions to Canadian identity include describing and mapping the mountain ranges and waterways, providing remedies and ways to heal, and administering rural economies such as fishing and crafting with fine materials. The land continues to shape the culture here, and visitors are encouraged to respect the land, share goals of sustainability, and revitalize eco-friendly opportunities among the wildlife.

Algonquian, Blackfoot, and Haida are only a few languages spoken among the indigenous communities who call Canada home. French and English represent two out of the most prominent eleven languages spoken in the family of vernaculars. When it comes to the ratio between the median earnings of an indigenous person and the rest of the population, that figure continues to rise among other demographics and averages higher than $70,000 in western Canada. In 2017, over 370,000 indigenous students worked toward a degree or a post-secondary diploma. While the education gap has significantly decreased, this does not help in the understanding of why indigenous employment rates – which tend to decrease in Alberta among different communities and appear to be strikingly low – plummeted after a long improvement. For Smudging, visit the City of Medicine Hat for events such as the AUMA Smart Cities Challenge or participate in Canadian Heritage Week featuring a variety of guest speakers.

CHAPTER 4

The Canadian Constitution and Political System

The head of state of Canada is the sovereign of the United Kingdom, King Edward VIII. By virtue of the Statute of Westminster (1931) and other documents, international relations between the said state and Canada are not regulated. At the federal level, the provinces also have the same state as they all share among provinces. As of 2011, there are 308 deputies in the Canadian Parliament. The federal government of Canada is led by the prime minister, who is appointed by the governor-general. Neither the House of the Prime Minister nor the Cabinet is elected directly by the people. Contrary to popular belief, Canada is not a parliamentary republic.

The Canadian Constitution has two parts, the Constitution Act (Constitution Act, 1867 and 1982) and the Constitution. It includes the Canada Act of 1982, adopted by the British Parliament at the request of the Canadian Parliament and with the consent of eight out of ten provinces. According to the first paragraph of the Constitution Act of 1867, it declared the second one as Canada's rightful act and ordered the Parliament of the United Kingdom to pass it. That is, the act of the United Kingdom continued to serve as a piece of internal Canadian legislation and could only be modified by the United Kingdom Parliament itself. The Constitution Act of 1982 introduced the final algorithm for changes. It can only be amended by the British Parliament at the request of all parties concerned. In fact, there is only one amendment, the repetition in 1997 of the addition of Newfoundland and Labrador to Newfoundland, Nova Scotia, New Brunswick, and PPI. The rest of the time since 1982, the constitutional review process has been terminated.

CHAPTER 5

Canada's Provinces and Territories: Unique Charact

Canada is comprised of 10 provinces and 3 territories, each with its own unique features. They are (from east to west): Newfoundland and Labrador, Prince Edward Island, Nova Scotia, New Brunswick, Quebec, Ontario, Manitoba, Saskatchewan, Alberta, British Columbia, Yukon Territory, Northwest Territories, and Nunavut. The people of the St. Lawrence seal this entry as sailors depart the Maritime provinces in New Brunswick and Nova Scotia on open waters leading to Newfoundland and Labrador. The diverse provinces of Canada are unified by breathtaking landscapes that stretch from coast to coast. Newfoundland and Labrador, along with Prince Edward Island, New Brunswick, and Nova Scotia, make up the eastern region of Canada, sharing the same Maritime Culture.

Together, these provinces offer visitors a chance to experience the rich heritage of Canada with their strong ties to the sea. Moving inland, Quebec offers a blending of old-world charm with new-age technologies and architecture in its largest cities of Montreal and Quebec City. Ontario is the heartland of this Canadian nation, abutting with gorgeous natural forests and the Great Lakes. Manitoba and Saskatchewan, long seen as prairie provinces, are quite attractive with the largest nature park in Canada, Atikaki Provincial Park, located in the north of Winnipeg. With the Rocky Mountains, Alberta is famous for Jasper National Park and Banff National Park. The west coast of Canada is mainly dominated by British Columbia and is known for its scenic beauty and coal mining industry. The highest peak of the coastal mainland, Mount Waddington, lies around 250 kilometers away from the Lanstone in the Pacific Ranges of the Coast Mountains. Yukon, Northwest Territories, and Nunavut form the upper north of Canada, a portion of the Canadian landscape that is often referred to as the Canadian North, separated from the southern part by a coastline in the Arctic Ocean.

CHAPTER 6

The Role of French and English Languages in Canadi

Canada's origins are incredibly multicultural, a fact reflected within the country's linguistic environment. Today, Canada officially recognizes French and English, Canada's two 'founding peoples,' as the official languages of the country. In addition, many Canadians speak languages that have little to do with Canada's colonial past. About 7 million Canadians, for example, speak neither French nor English. Hebrew, Chinese, Italian, German, Spanish, and Portuguese are among the most common of these languages. Creole languages, including Inuktitut and Gwich'in, are spoken by Canada's indigenous peoples and are descended from lingua francas, or trade languages, used by First Nations long before Europeans arrived.

Today, more than 80% of Canada's population uses English and about 20% uses French. The role of English has its roots in pre-Confederation Canada, specifically in territories that would ultimately become the English-speaking provinces. Since English-speaking territories were the first to join Canada, the country's infrastructure and systems (including educational, legal, and parliamentary systems) were English. When the Canadian Confederation occurred in 1867, many in the newly formed country expected that all new Canadian citizens would, and should, speak English. Normatively, while jealously preserving their own language, citizens of other 'new countries' have moved through this stage. In Canada, however, linguistic duality has remained important not just as a historical memento of two groups' feuding over accents and point of origin but as a reflection of the economic and cultural power of French-speaking Quebeckers. Political concessions (i.e., the 1867 British North American Act granting Quebeckers an "opting out" clause from section 93 of the BNA act) betray an uneasy alliance between Quebec and Canada.

CHAPTER 7

Canada's Economy: Industries and Trade Partners

Canada is a global anomaly of peace, prosperity, and cooperative diversity. In order to understand the nature of Canadian culture - with its myriad of peoples indelibly etched against and within a vast yet fragile ecosystem - it is important to be familiar with the economy and its major industries that shape it.

The industries that have driven the Canadian economy can be divided neatly by region and natural resource concern. Although fresh-water ecosystems and the agricultural industry associated with their production contribute significantly to the economy, the focus shall be limited here primarily to secondary industries of manufacturing, energy, and resource extraction that have dominated Canadian economic history and currently contribute the greatest economic activity since the mid-nineteenth century. It is important to remember that Canada encourages foreign investment in the country and some of the largest businesses in Canada are under foreign ownership and control. Canada is a 'trading nation' with a very strong export industry. This makes Canada vulnerable to world markets and world economies. Canada's two most important trading partners are the United States and Mexico. All 3 countries are involved in a strong trading relationship ranging from industrial goods, energy products, to agricultural products. These trading activities have been made possible by the North American Free Trade Agreement (NAFTA). Additionally, Canada is also a strong trading partner with Japan and the countries that make up the EU (European Union). The main product export during 2015 were vehicles/automobiles, crude oil, machinery, electricity, pulp and paper and wooden products. This demonstrates that Canada maintains a strong emphasis on manufacturing and natural resource extraction/production.

CHAPTER 8

Canadian Arts and Literature: Influences and Notab

The country now known as Canada has been the site of a human presence for thousands of years. Abounding in people and cultures that trace their ancestry to nearly every continent, the story of Canada weaves together a great many threads to create a richly diverse society in which each member is eager to share their unique heritage.

Canada is home to a vast array of arts and literatures. Writers, painters, photographers, and sculptors have all been influenced by Canada's diverse landscapes and cultures, canvassing its cities, coasts, forests, prairies, and tundra. Indigenous and immigrant artists portray their insights into the human world and the nation, each contribution an important thread in the cultural fabric of the nation. Canadian arts and literature reflect Canada's subtle, sometimes conflicting, chapters of human habitation on the land, as well as the disorientation and delight of the modern world's struggles, cultures, and events. Arts from non-English speaking Quebec, Aboriginal/French Canada, and the many cultural communities have also greatly influenced the world's understanding of Canada's complex identity and what it means to be Canadian.

Festivals, performances, visual arts, writings, and art expression from across Canada are showcased in many cities, from world's fairs in and beyond Canada, and at international literary events and gatherings. Torontonian Northrop Frye is considered one of the most important literary theorists of his time. Vincent Massey, the first Canadian to serve as Governor of Canada, and his brother, novelist and Governor General of Canada, 1967-73, the Rt. Hon. Vincent Massey served, through individual practices and actions, to encourage the arts and expansion of Canadians' understandings of their heritage. Many generations of immigrants, including both parents from where I come from, immigrated to Canada and shared their hopes and fears, traditions, and their insights into Canadian life in their poetry and visual arts. Such individuals, and the practices of the world's artists, help to create Canada's and the investors worldwide and in a great many variety of transactions whose place the federal, provincial, and territorial governments work to protect and advance.

CHAPTER 9

Exploring Canada's Natural Wonders: National Parks

Canada is located on the North American continent and, with only two exceptions, shares border areas with the United States of America. With its multiple coastal and riverine areas and sub-Arctic forests, it is no surprise that there are seven national parks and three marine conservation zones around the territory to actively protect Canada's rich ecology. That also extends to the hundreds of migratory bird sanctuaries and habitat conservation areas that are maintained around the country by largely consent of the landowners.

In terms of wildlife more generally, Canada faces many of the same issues as the rest of the world in that it is attempting to conserve the diversity and numbers of its native species. To that end, Canada has 1523 species at risk based on population size and habitat protection, as per its Species At Risk Public Registry. Those threatened with annexation are labelled as 'endangered' and are given a red background and dark grey text, while those threatened with demotion are labelled as 'not at risk' and are given a light and dark shading effect. Among the species at risk in Canada are 34 bird species, 6 of which are considered to be 'endangered'—at imminent risk of becoming extinct.

Canada's natural features include seven miles of alpine passes in the Canadian Rockies, which are a popular tourist destination particularly among mountaineering and backpacking enthusiasts. Additionally, Canada's National Parks are home to 43 heritage landmarks and have been included as a part of a UNESCO-designated World Heritage Site. Other natural attractions include Niagara Falls, Dinosaur Provincial Park, the Northern Lights, Bay of Fundy (the world's highest tides), and Saguenay-St. Lawrence Marine Park. The shores of the country also serve as important sanctuaries and breeding areas for a great many bird species, including pelican, heron, and swan species. A great number of migratory bird species, from grebes to raptors, transit Canadian airspace on an annual basis between their Arctic and Antarctic grounds.

CHAPTER 10

The Arctic Region: Climate, Wildlife, and Indigeno

This refers to the north of 60 degrees latitude and is the most northerly of Canada's physiographic regions. A definition of the area by the Arctic Environmental Statement is the area north of the approximate treeline, customary hunting area boundaries to the North Pole. Over 141 million barrels of oil were shipped from the Port of Pointers through the Mackenzie Delta in October 2003. The earth's axis is inclined at 66 degrees and is the reason for the existence of these regions. The tilt of the earth allows the sun to stay continuously above the horizon for a period of over 24 hours during the summer solstice. It is this tilt of the earth that allows areas to experience continuous day/night. The earth is tilted to an angle equal to the latitude of the Arctic Circle, this is in turn why the tropics are called the Tropic of Cancer and Tropic of Capricorn (sun tropics from the poles towards the equator).

Environment Climate: The Territorial Environmental Agency in the Northwest Territories classifies the climate as a sub-Arctic cold desert. This classification is based on both continuous and discontinuous permafrost, low precipitation (50 mm/year), less than 100 frost-free days, flash flooding, and rapid melting of snow during the short spring.

Wildlife: The region is home to a multitude of wildlife that are able to survive in the harsh environment. There are a few creatures that can only be found in the Arctic region. These species include the Polar Bear, Muskox, Peary Caribou, Grizzly Bear, Barren Ground Grizzly Bear, the Arctic Fox, and several nesting grounds of birds such as the Snowy Owl and the Willow Ptarmigan. The Arctic has the longest migrating caribou herds in the world; both the Beverly caribou and the Porcupine caribou travel in Southeast and Yukon Alaska. Hungry northern herds find their way to Norton Sound and chew the lichen from the rocky islands of Kotzebue.

Indigenous Communities: The sparsely populated region is home to Inuit and First Nations People. The Inuit are found pretty much throughout most of the Arctic from Greenland-Canada to Alaska. Evidence has shown that Inuit and other First Nations have lived in the Arctic for 4000 years. Today, the coastal communities rely primarily on hunting (marine and terrestrial life), fishing, trapping, and tourism. Sea ice, rivers, and glaciers are important transport modes for harvesters and residents. Approximately 29,000 Inuit live in the Canadian Arctic today, the Inuit are found in different areas of the Arctic: Inuit (Canadian Arctic), Kalaallit (western Greenlandic), and Iñupiat, Inuvialuit, and Yup'ik in Alaska. The Inuit inhabit 53 communities in the three territories. Although the Beaufort is home to significant oil and gas development (Mackenzie Delta, Hibernia), the estimated 5,000-6,000 Inuit of the region are predominantly a hunting population.

CHAPTER 11

The Rocky Mountains: Geology, Flora, and Outdoor A

Formed over 80 million years ago, the Rocky Mountains stretch more than 4,000 kilometers from northern Alaska in North America to the southwestern United States. Many Canadian visitors are amazed by the Rocky Mountains during their first visit; the sight often evokes a sense of awe and appreciation for the greatness of Canada. Geologists believe that the Rockies were created when the North American Plate collided with another large landmass (called Laurentia) millions of years ago, creating large rock ridges. Two of Canada's Rockies—the northern and southern Rockies—surround Alberta from Jasper in the north to Waterton in the south; they are located in the western part of the province. Thousands of tourists from around the world come to the Canadian Rockies every year to enjoy their natural beauty and engage in outdoor activities such as hiking, backpacking, mountaineering, wildlife watching, fishing, cycling, golfing, skiing, skating, and snowshoeing.

Southern Alberta hosts Waterton Lakes National Park, which borders the United States and is a World Heritage region called the Waterton-Glacier International Peace Park. Among the town's streets, diverse wildflowers, plant life, and bird species inhabit Waterton Lakes National Park. The Rockies are home to a diverse range of mammals, including wolves, grizzly bears, mountain goats, marmots, lynx, wolverines, pikas, and a special subpopulation of elk. As well, many tourists have seen elk, moose, mountain sheep, deer, and bear. Despite the apparent tough and uninhabitable lands, the Rockies are home to many thriving plant communities that have adapted to mountain life and that come alive with color in the spring and summer months. In fact, the Rockies are home to Mediterranean grasslands and the northern boundary of a layer of rainforest. To better protect the Rockies' beauty and animal species, over a million hectares of the world's most famous and true representatives of nature have been protected in 10 national parks and 3 provincial parks in Alberta and British Columbia.

CHAPTER 12

The Great Lakes: Ecosystems, Shipping, and Recreat

The Great Lakes are the world's largest group of freshwater lakes, boasting a combination of volume, connectivity, and biodiversity unmatched by any other group of lakes on Earth. They contain over 20% of the world's surface fresh water and 80% of North America's supply, yet while remaining some of the youngest and most productive ecosystems, the waters were among the most drastically affected by industrialization. They are home to diverse ecosystems and wildlife, including more than 140 fish species, and have had a significantly impacted shoreline, but recovery efforts are proving successful. The Great Lakes' ecosystem and status as an international border make them of great economic and environmental significance, with shipping potentially posing the risk of introducing non-native aquatic species. The lakes support numerous communities and provide recreational opportunities for millions of residents and visitors.

Shipping on the Great Lakes was the catalyst for the settlement and growth of the region. As the US grew, maritime traffic on the lakes grew. The opening of the Saint Lawrence Seaway in 1959 connected the Great Lakes to the Atlantic Ocean, and the development of larger ships has continued to increase shipping on the lakes. The historical growth of cities and industry around the lakes has significantly affected the landscape and interactions with the ecosystem, but there are many opportunities along the shores for visitors to connect with natural, cultural, and historical sites. There are over 10,900 miles of shoreline for visitors to explore, including more than 5,200 miles of open coast along the northern shores of Lake Superior and Lake Michigan. Coastal areas are important stops for migratory birds and offer nesting sites for waterfowl. Development in the Great Lakes region has resulted in significant alterations to the ecosystem, but multiple sites have been preserved for visitors to connect with the wild and scenic nature of the lakes.

CHAPTER 13

The Atlantic Provinces: Fisheries, Culture, and To

The area of Canada from the Atlantic and Great Lakes to the Arctic is even more diverse in landscape, climate, and society. Newfoundland and Labrador, Prince Edward Island, Nova Scotia, and New Brunswick all have extensive shorelines and their economies and cultures are associated with Atlantic fishing and the tourist appeal of the unique coastal setting and relatively unresource-industrialized environment. Although the value of oil and natural gas coming ashore from the Atlantic offshore is greater than that of the fish just offshore, the populations of Newfoundland, P.E.I. and Cape Breton, as practically, as entirely dependent on "The Fishery" as they were when Cabot fishing voyages brought Europeans into the region more than 500 years ago.

The Atlantic Provinces are also each different. Diverse First Nations communities and a growing number of newcomers are changing small towns, big cities, and the countryside in the eastern part of Canada. The fresh air, land, and water along the Atlantic coasts and the comfort of living are the main attractions for lots of people who don't live in the Provinces and who sometimes come for a visit. When they do, they help make the staples of local economies like seafood, golf, beaches, and nature walking relatively profitable and make others, like historical museum preserves, boat tours, and cultural celebrations at least breaking even.

CHAPTER 14

The Pacific Coast: Rainforests, Marine Life, and I

The Pacific Coast encompasses a series of dramatic and inviting landscapes that manage the constraints of the narrow isthmus which serves as the seam of the country's main transportation corridor. It features a chain of mountain ranges, main river valleys, and deep fjords, providing a picturesque relationship between the land and the sea. Abundant and diverse marine life, from the humble groundfish such as halibut to the immense marine mammals such as killer whales (orca) and sea lions, inhabit coastal waters on their seasonal migrations, often just moments away from exquisite sandy beaches. With its illustrious temperate rainforests, episodic Pacific storms, extraordinary tidal fluctuations, and dynamic living cultures, the Pacific Coast is a place of epic adventure and grand exploration.

For the most part, the Pacific Coast is comprised of the traditional territories of the Indigenous peoples, including the Inuit, who engaged in trade, diplomacy, and war for millennia. As the largest group of Indigenous Peoples on the coast, the Coast Salish tenaciously maintain their presence in major urban centers like Vancouver and Seattle, as well as in remote locations on the northern tip of Vancouver Island and among the rugged islands that rest in the middle of the Strait of Georgia. In former times and right now, the indigenous peoples of Canada's west coast have carved a legacy of crusade in BC, Oregon, Hawaii, Alaska, onward Canada's Arctic Coast, and the Americas. Over the many centuries and presently, the many Coast Salish groups continue to have an undeniable influence and prominence over the multinational borderlands, coastal communities, and cosmopolitan elites who now call this place day and home.

CHAPTER 15

Urban Centers in Canada: Toronto, Montreal, Vancou

From coast to coast, Canada is punctuated by some of the most breathtaking as well as underappreciated cities in the world. Toronto is renowned for being one of the most multicultural cities, not in Canada, or even North America, but the world. Here, the city's official motto, "Diversity Our Strength," embodies the people, events, spiritualities, food, and clothing of hundreds of various cultural communities. Bordered by the Atlantic Ocean, Montreal is the largest city in Quebec, as well as its most populous metropolis. Its old town is constructed in the 17th and 18th century buildings and attracts between 14 and 18 million people every year. Ontario is Canada's corporate and cultural center, home to approximately 10 million people who can participate in a variety of events, activities, and customs.

To originate from or simply to live in Toronto is to represent hundreds of various cultures, every religion, 140 languages, and hundreds more dialects. Vancouver was chosen as the world's third-best city in the Economist Intelligence Unit's list of the best cities to live in 2019. It may be known for its extraordinary and varied communities, with food offerings from Indian and Syrian bakers known as Kootenay Soulfood to any visitors, particularly Canadian. It's a mixed-race city situated between the Pacific Ocean and the North Shore Mountains, known for its boating, Stanley Park, cultural life, and beautiful scenery. You may also go SUP boarding and whale-watching off the shore of English Bay. Many of the restaurants provide creatively designed, juicy meals using the best local products on the planet. In addition, the best Canadian beer producers are located throughout the city, emphasizing hoppy beers that are hot, cold, or canned.

CHAPTER 16

Multiculturalism in Canada: Immigration Patterns a

Canada is an immigrant country in which a very high proportion of the people are the direct descendants of immigrants. Multiculturalism as a lived reality is writ large in Canadian cities. Immigration patterns have varied over time; immigration was primarily European in the first half of the last century, but has since 1960 become more and more diverse, with parallel waves of refugees and family class migrants joining those in the economic category. The patterns of the last couple of decades are helping to enhance the diversity of the population. A full seventy percent or more of newcomers are visible minorities hailing from Asia, Africa, and the Middle East, representing a wide range of religions, languages, and cultures. Multiculturalism as a policy for the country was first declared by the Trudeau government in the 1970s and quickly became a point of pride for many in the country. The policy centers around the federal government's refusal to allocate or endorse one national culture as superior or more primary than another. At its best, Canada is a multiculturalism "mosaic" rather than a "melting pot" of culturally diverse parts rather than one homogeneous whole.

Communities in Canada are where the details come together in the concrete fabric of life, gesturing toward "multicultural interactions at a grass-roots level, sensory immediacy, and the physicality of realization." There are more than 200 ethno-cultural communities in western Canada, including a substantial Aboriginal population made up of three groups: status and non-status Treaty and non-Treaty Indians, Métis, and Inuit. In short, western Canadians experience culture on a day-to-day basis in their relationships with neighbors; their engagement in cultural activities; in friendship with émigrés, refugees, and community members with family ties extending transnationally; and in their very presence as individuals of cultural and ethnic diversity. Canada's population's tapestry is a diverse one, but the individual threads are woven into the larger communal fabric, the shared responsibilities of citizenship and loyalty that make the nation as a whole a potent mix of tolerance and difference. The intricacy of languages, religious practices, aesthetic tastes, and daily activities across a country of great expanse has encouraged a significant national character of acceptance and coexistence of multiple cultural streams despite common challenges related to racialization, racism, and resulting marginalization, particularly in urban centers.

CHAPTER 17

Education in Canada: Schools, Universities, and Re

Schooling is compulsory in Canada up to the age of 16 or 18, depending on the province. Education is mandated at the provincial level, with provincial governments funding public education throughout elementary, middle, and secondary school, as well as educational programming. The government also funds a portion of the expenses of university fees. An extensive system of public colleges offers training and diploma programs that are generally shorter-term and focused on vocational and technical skills for welding, hospitality, tourism, journalism, criminal justice, law enforcement, as well as many other occupational categories. Canada's universities study and research in the typical humanities, social sciences, and pure and applied sciences, as well as in the professional fields of engineering, law, medicine, dentistry, nursing, rehabilitation medicine, and teaching. Women and non-binary teachers have a major presence at Canadian universities, and there has been a concerted effort by many universities over the last two decades to recruit and retain these groups onto their faculties. About 4,500 university professors have a Native American, Inuit, or Métis background in all, and dedicated Early

Career and Master's programs at most universities have produced significant numbers of Aboriginal and Indigenous health professionals and all of the other professional services.

Canadian universities are research-intensive and are required to produce original work. They are also centers of excellence around the world for advanced study and are expected to work with the communities they serve to produce new knowledge and improve life. Since 1996, there has been a cooperative inter-university approach to research called the Canadian University Sector Review, and two percent of textile spending has paid for an umbrella organization to coordinate this project. Since 1998, all research projects have been conducted according to the principles of entrepreneurship, internships, and innovation. The focus is on people as well as knowledge transfer and assessment. Each year, the Association of Universities and Colleges of Canada licenses a flag that distinguishes research- and teaching-intensive universities from other colleges that are more focused on career training. 25,000 visas are issued annually to international researchers of all levels of seniority, according to the Business, Trade, and Investment board of all the Foreign Embassies. On one-third of working days, an international peace and security speaker from a foreign university was to be found at a lecture on peace and security studies at a Canadian university. Reputational rankings of Canadian universities are offered by Maclean's Magazine and the Higher Education Evaluation Council of Canada. Universities seek national and international reputation for their research and for the quality of their graduates, and there has been a growing participation by Canadian universities in world rankings. Universities are also ranked by their provincial governments.

CHAPTER 18

Healthcare System in Canada: Universal Coverage an

The healthcare system in Canada is based on the idea that all people should have access to personal and family healthcare, regardless of illness or social status or financial standing, and as such it is noted for its universal coverage. Public efforts in health and health care result in Canada's low rate of socioeconomic disparities in health and the high degree of health achieved by Canadians. This is an important feature of our wider society - that we try to avoid extremes of wealth and poverty, and that as a basic humanitarian provision, everyone should have access to necessary medical care, disability benefits, and other forms of social support. We believe that, though everyone can rise to success by their own efforts, no one in a civilized society should needlessly be allowed to fall to the lowest rank. We all have an interest in this because we might ourselves become sick or injured; and we all are bound together and sustained by a web of mutual support and cooperation.

Healthcare and healthcare professionals are some of the foundational elements in a community that contribute to social and political order and stability. Alongside other fields that are more obviously connected to social order like law, teaching, policing, social services, etc., healthcare assurance ensures basic wellness and adds to the overall smooth functioning of any society. Whole societies come together to help the wounded and distressed and to maintain the smooth functioning of social and economic systems in which each has to play a part. We also believe that, as a group of generally good-natured people, the Canadians would help a neighbor in health, because he is a part of the seamless order of the Canadian fabric. We seek community building, and the healthcare system is not just about individual saving and improving but also an organized, rational effort to preserve and build each nation's health and general well-being. Whole communities have an important stake in the varieties of expertise that contribute to the healthier lives they want to build.

CHAPTER 19

Canadian Cuisine: Regional Specialties and Influen

Like its population, Canadian cuisine is a melting pot consisting of an abundance of regional specialties and global influences. From fish and chips—particularly popular in many of Canada's Atlantic provinces—to the authentic Inuit cuisine brimming with seal, whale, and caribou, Canadian dining possibilities are very diverse. In Quebec (pronounced Quebec), the French settlers' legacy remains strong in such dishes as soupe aux pois (pea soup with large pieces of ham), relishes, brown sugar pie, and tourtière (a meat pie).

In Southern Ontario, ethnic influence from the area's Dutch and German settlers is present in dishes such as weiner schnitzel, which remains a popular fare at Oktoberfest celebrations. The same area—along with other parts of Canada—can also dine on reformed pigs' feet, dive into a Plum Duff (a steamed pudding), enjoy butter tarts, assorted jams, and try in hot chocolate 'Timbits', which are donut holes. The Prairies and western provinces feature increasingly popular multicultural cuisine, but big North American steaks, bison, and other game remain a dinner staple. Wild blueberries are a favorite ingredient in hors d'oeuvres and desserts, and wild rice is sometimes served with game dishes. Bannock (also known as Indian bread) is often eaten not only on the prairies but in the North as well. In British Columbia, a focus on seafood is influenced by Asian cuisine located on the coast. Chicken and shrimp salads, sushi, Vietnamese spring rolls, and pan-Asian noodle bowls all grace family dining tables in this area. For an idea more widespread throughout the country, Canadians enjoy taking a piece of ham and topping it with pineapple and then broiling. Failing ham, it's often shrimp.

CHAPTER 20

Sports and Recreation in Canada: Popular Activitie

Sports and Recreation in Canada: Popular Activities and Events
To celebrate the unique landscape of the country, Canada has promoted sports on snow, ice, and water as a major pastime. On a per capita basis, it spends among the most practicing winter sports in the world. Equipment and services for the sports specific to the country are, consequently, extensively bought not only by natives but also by many foreigners across the nation.

Winter sports are big, especially skiing. The country is one of the world's big ski centers, drawing people watching the sports as well as riding on the trails. The country is also the site of the world's fastest cross-country ski race.

Attended by large numbers of tourists and widely publicized, the competitions throughout Canada are often held. Outstanding winter sports teams steadily compete internationally and represent Canada. Just before the Olympic games, Canadian athletes from time to time attend warm-up competitions, and their performance is generally high. Also, Canada stays in the forefront.

Canadian sports reflect the diverse mix of citizens playing modern and traditional sports. Through their recreation choices, communities express local values. Rugby, cricket, football, and hockey are common. The favorite sport in Canada is hockey, and every night, kids and adults can be found on ice rinks playing their version of the world's favorite hockey game. It is the national winter season and is taught in schools across the nation in sports programs. Highly pursued for young hockey players from hockey academies, however, few join the professional hockey team. While extremely talented, ice hockey and figure skaters may also face a shortage of financial help. Soccer and gymnastics are also generally taught at college.

CHAPTER 21

Transportation in Canada: Roads, Railways, and Air

- Canada's topography, culture, and climate create a wide range of travel challenges and requirements. As a geographically huge, personally dispersed country, Canada has evolved a transportation system that is responsive to both its wide range of physical characteristics and the country's demographics. The Canadian road system provides relatively easy transportation access to within about 100 km of 90% of the population. The extensive Trans-Canada Highway permits Canadians to get wherever there needs to be handled. A total of 900,000 km of national, provincial, and territorial roadways weave Canada together in a connected transportation network. Canada has nearly 4 million kilometers of roads and ranks number 30 in the world in terms of the percentage of roads paved. Roads managed by provincial or territorial governments contribute nearly 4 ½ times the number of road kilometers when compared to the national road network. Over 11 million cars, 760,000 campers, 2 ½ million trucks, and 36,000 motorcycles navigate Canada's roadways annually.

- With 72,961 kilometers of track, Canada has the world's 2nd largest rail network after China. Canada's rail system provides shippers and industry a vital link to port facilities and other means of trans-shipment. More than one quarter of Canadian rail freight arrives at or departs from a port facility. Canada has about 3,500 public and private airports and heliports, of which about 600 have regular passenger services. Air travel is also a major highway alternative in Canada, such that there are currently just over 600,000 licensed general aviation pilots in Canada. The national transportation system can provide mobile and instant dissemination of information, people and products across the country into and out of Canada.

CHAPTER 22

Environmental Issues in Canada: Climate Change and

Canada is one of the most developed countries in the world, and as such, it also has a high per capita consumption of resources. As of 2008, the per capita ecological footprint of Canadians was 7.6 global hectares (gha), while as of 2006, the emissions of greenhouse gases averaged 22,922 megatonnes of CO2 equivalent. These factors, combined with the very limited portion of arable land (7.2% of total Canada) that is actually in use and the significant percentage of natural forest and lands that are under conservation, make it clear why the main environmental issues facing Canada today are climate change and conservation. It is important to note that climate change has been taking place in the region for the last 12,000 years, but the rate and scale of change that has happened in recent years are of a different magnitude altogether.

Temperature: The average temperature in Canada has been increasing at a rate of about 0.9°C per decade, twice as high as the global temperature. Scientists have said that if emission rates continue the way they are, there will be an increase of 2-4°C by the year 2050. This can result in more frequent and severe heat waves, affecting human health and the environment. It also has the potential to cause relatively small adaptations in the way of living, such as the consumption of more energy for cooling. The summer of 2005 saw a number of such occurrences hit Canada, especially affecting British Columbia and the Maritimes. It is also estimated that by the end of the century, the summers in Prince George, British Columbia, will get two degrees hotter and could last more than half a year.

CHAPTER 23

Indigenous Rights and Reconciliation in Canada

For centuries, across Turtle Island, indigenous nations of Canada have existed, developed, and retained their languages and cultural traditions. Many of these nations have systems of governance based on treaties or other agreements with the British Crown and other colonial powers. Today in Canada, the term "indigenous" refers to the three distinct groups of people—First Nations, Métis, and Inuit—who are descended from those who inhabited the land for many generations and continue to be deeply connected to their cultural values and territories. As a multicultural and diverse country, Canada embodies a range of ethnic, cultural, linguistic, and religious groups.

For more than a century, Canada echoed a policy of centralization that aimed to assimilate indigenous people by destroying their communities, languages, cultural practices, and spiritual beliefs. Located in downtown Toronto, the Canadian Museum for Human Rights (CMHR) features indigenous rights and reconciliation as one of five galleries that explore the challenges faced by the right of freedom and community, indigenous rights in Canada, and the citizen-based vehicles for social change, such as the example of the adoptive roots. Home to one of the oldest legal traditions in the world (dating back to the Iroquois Confederacy), indigenous people seek to move forward towards reconciliation, highlighting through the important lessons learned from history and humanity's futures, this gallery critical message for Canadians to become more aware and responsible, developing a more cohesive and just society. The reconciliation process reveals a society's moral compass and mirrors the very fabric of our society.

CHAPTER 24

International Relations: Canada's Role in Global A

Canada has been called a "soft power," a term which refers to a narrative that defines Canada as a compassionate, caring, generous, and open-minded country that has a valuable role to play on the global scene. Throughout Canada's history, special emphasis has been placed on the country's relationships with others. Canada's role in global affairs has taken many forms, ranging from our work in international diplomacy (diplomacy is the practice of conducting negotiations between representatives of states or groups) and United Nations peacekeeping to our involvement in trade negotiations and responses to immigration and refugees. Our work among our international partners builds upon Canada's historical ties and looks toward the future. The result is a foreign policy that directly reflects Canadian interests, history, and values. Joseph Nye, a political scientist and former U.S. government official who has held influential security and military roles, coined the term "soft power" in the 1990s and went on to publish a book about Canada itself. Nye described Canada as a "soft power superpower" and suggested that the country serves as a model for "smart power," a savvy blend of military and soft power. Today, Canada uses "smart power" to balance its reliance on the "hard" (military) power of its neighbor and largest trading partner, the United States. It is a philosophy that takes advantage of Canada's international reputation as a peacekeeper and good global citizen. Overall, Canada has an international reputation that is rooted in British and European concepts of democratic peace and the rule of law.

When Canada was first developed as a nation, it was a British colony that had the stated intention of preserving the "British way of life." In order to achieve this, Canada sought to set itself apart from the United States by being all the things the U.S. was not: orderly, peaceful, and polite. Additionally, the country embraced the exchange and integration of many cultures, a practice that became overwhelming the moment there were more non-British settlers than British settlers in the country. Many political commentators have suggested that peacekeeping is a "manifest destiny" for Canadians. By this, it is meant that because of Canada's geography, history, and resources, Canadians have a moral imperative as a "responsible peacekeeper." However, we have demonstrated such a strong interest in fighting for peace in recent years that it is difficult, if not impossible, to pinpoint exactly where our "manifest destiny" to be peacekeepers came from. From a legal point of view, Canada has the power to assist in the establishment of international security. At the international level, Canada can draw on consensual influence as a tool of soft power. Inside the country, the official policies and actions of Canada are often influenced by people and organizations in which consensual power is vested. In some cases, Canada's defense policy adheres to its beliefs. However, there is also the development of Canadian force options that dramatically depart from the prevailing view in Canada, raising questions about the power and influence of consensual power in a democratic society enshrined in a liberal justice-based system.

CHAPTER 25

Innovations and Technologies in Canada: Achievemen

In recent years, innovation has been making rapid strides. As a result, more and more technology companies are being classified as "ridesharing" or "home sharing" companies. Canada has also seen significant technical advances in recent years, and there are no signs of this trend slowing down. This post will examine some of Canada's accomplishments and the discovery and future trend for different technologies.

The world today is currently grappling with the fourth industrial revolution. On May 7, 2019, the Royal Bank of Canada (RBC) announced in a report that Canada needs to embrace its fourth industrial revolution (also known as AI economy) to grow its tech industry from a CA$12 billion to a CA$300 billion behemoth in 2023. The RBC report points out that Canada was the first country in the world to develop good-quality AI infrastructure, evident by the country's close partnership with the Silicon Valley-based OpenAI, which played a key role in the development of the GPT-3 language model, which has proven to be game-changing, said the report. Canada can become a world leader because of this, by deepening our investment in AI, connected technology, and climate change adaptation across all regions of the economy, creating 12 million jobs in the current decade. The report went as far as to call this the next "moonshot". RBC is predicting four fields will be primarily the "other driver" of the fourth industrial revolution including quantum computers, AI, nanotechnology, and IIOT. RBC predicts that Canada also has a chance in those fields, well-acquainted in research scientist expertise in those fields, making up a larger share of the worker population than conventional technology and software development. By embracing each of these technology areas to 2040, Canada's Tech and ICT Economy are expected to grow: Quantum computers by 2050, from $12.6 billion in 2021 to $96 billion in 2041. Artificial intelligence by 2050, from $22.2 billion in 2021 to $559 billion in 2041. Nanotechnology by 2050, from $1.6 billion in 2021 to $695.7 billion in 2041. IIoT by 2050, from $6.5 billion in 2021 to $1.51 trillion in 2041.

CHAPTER 26

The Canadian Identity: Values, Symbols, and Nation

What does it mean to be Canadian? The essence of Canadian identity lies in the values, symbols that reflect those values, and the pride that inspires a personal and profound commitment to these values. Many symbols define the nature of the nation, and the ones most commonly associated with Canada are perhaps the natural ones: the maple leaf, the beaver, and the many geographic features in the U.S.-Canadian border that have been immortalized in the music of Canadian songwriters.

Today, the Canada-U.S. border symbolizes the great differences between the two countries. When asked to choose a Canadian symbol, 85 percent of Canadians point to the maple leaf as a source of pride, and among those who selected the leaf, 91 percent are at least 45 years old and are significantly more likely than younger adults to hold this attitude. The lack of consensus suggests that the nation does not have a single "official" symbol; Canadian identity is defined much more by values and institutions that are tied to the nation. However, an analysis of the data shows that there are three separate Canadian value systems that are commonly held in public opinion as well as among our political and corporate leaders. The traditional least-defining Canadian values are those celebrating the virtues of thrift, humility, sharing, getting ahead through hard work, never complaining, and generally illustrating deference and conservatism. Moreover, they are the values least connected to the other two percent of Canadians, whereas other U.S.-like values are held in equal measure by French and English and by all regions. In exceptional ways, the Canadian mosaic continues to define who we are as individuals and as a nation and what makes "us" different from everyone else. The Canadian mosaic, like Canadian values, can mean different things to different people, as long as the result is inclusive, Canadians must be anchored in values.

CHAPTER 27

Conclusion: Reflecting on Canada's Past, Present,

Taking the time to reflect on the exploration that has been conducted into the diverse landscapes and cultures of Canada, the logical conclusion is to return to the sea, where the whole attempt began. The assignment provided a challenging opportunity to consider the different landscapes for inquiry and to touch down at a few of the airports connected to this investigation, providing only a brief sense of the small portion of Canada addressed by this exploration. From the Atlantic province cities of St. John's and Halifax to the western ports of Vancouver and Kelowna, to the fertile prairies of Winnipeg, through the great forests of the Prairies and Canadian Shield of the rural and resort communities surrounding Toronto, this exploration only touches the barest surfaces of the Canadian landscape. Inevitably, there is a sense of being incomplete and fragmented, trapped in norms that do not allow for an investigation quite as broad and deep as envisioned in the title of the research project. At the same time, what was touched upon allows for some historical, cultural, and insightful detail into the complex and exceeding diversities of the nation.

With that said, it is proposed that this exploration speaks to some of the variety of pasts woven into the signage and sounds that inflect Canada in the present tense. Through different eras of time, Canada was present in these physical and communal geographies: from the rural imaginaries of the Prairies and B.C. to the urban fixtures of memory in Halifax and St. John's. We may consider hardships of famine or expulsion, the genocides woven into the nation's history in St. John's, or the violence of colonization in Kelowna. That is often the way settler colonial nations are crafted, after all – through erasure and forgetting. Individual losses pile into a staggering number of netherworlds or half-worlds or worlds almost realized but not quite – they sit at the reserve itself. Yet, they are beginning to re-indigenize, from Winnipeg to Toronto, with the so-called red power that never disappeared but bristled to speak just under the skin of North America. It has been a story – or series of stories – with interminable beginnings and unfinished endings, but it represents a nation truly filled with potential retired in the souvenirs of its former glories, of former moments when belonging was less an abstract noun than a socialistic in your face.

www.ingramcontent.com/pod-product-compliance
Ingram Content Group UK Ltd.
Pitfield, Milton Keynes, MK11 3LW, UK
UKHW041826090225
454851UK00010B/155